Greek Gods

The Gods and Goddesses of Greek Mythology

Patrick Auerbach

© Copyright 2015 - All rights reserved.

Table of Contents

Introduction

Greek mythology is deeply ingrained in our culture. References to it are everywhere. In psychology we have the Oedipus complex and the opposition of Apollonian and Dionysian temperaments. In popular speech we describe epic journeys as odysseys, speak of other people 'opening Pandora's box' or 'having the golden touch,' and describe certain types of computer malware as 'Trojan horses.' Western literature and drama, of course, owe a deep debt to the Greek myths. Eugene O'Neill's *Mourning Becomes Electra* and Sartre's *The Flies* are two very different reinterpretations of the story of Orestes and Electra. Paul Frazer's Civil War novel *Cold Mountain* draws heavily on the Odyssey. Cocteau's *Orphee*, Rilke's *Sonnets to Orpheus* and Tennessee Williams' *Orpheus Descending* are all drawn from the same myth cycle.

It's difficult to draw up one comprehensive account of Greek mythology. Greek creation stories and accounts of the gods are many, varied and contradictory. Cultural understandings and religious practices changed, and the sacred stories shifted with them. When the Roman empire conquered the Greek lands they took over the Greek pantheon, renamed all the deities, and added in some stories of their own. What follows is an introduction to some of the common understandings of the gods and to some of the great cosmic and human stories that have left an enduring mark on our culture. Further reading suggestions are in the 'Sources' section at the end.

The Creation and the Gods

In The Beginning...

How did the world begin? The stories vary widely. One common feature is that the gods who reigned on Mount Olympus, the gods featured in the legends and the worship of the time, were the world's children, not its creators. In the beginning was chaos. From this chaos the first divine beings arose, and from their couplings life and order filled the void. But there was still plenty of chaos to go around. The ancient gods made war on each other, and there was great destruction before the Olympian gods arose and the world gained a precarious stability. Even the Olympians were hardly of one mind, and the wars of men were complicated, sometimes determined, by the power-struggles of the gods.

The Olympian creation myth, which was at some point the canonical version, says that in the beginning Gaia, the Earth, emerged from Chaos and, in her sleep, bore a son, Uranus, who ascended to the mountaintops and showered her with fertile rain; she conceived and bore other children--plants, beasts, birds, fish, one-eyed Cyclopes, hundred-handed Hecatoncheires, and also the Titans, the vast and powerful ancestors of the Olympian gods.

Uranus, wishing to maintain control of the world, imprisoned the Cyclopes and Hecatoncheires in the dark depths of Tartarus, far below the earth. Gaia was furious and encouraged the Titans, who were still free, to attack Uranus. Cronus, the boldest of them, did so, castrating him. Uranus either died or fled, predicting that Cronus also would be overthrown by his children. The splashing foam produced by Uranus' genitals and Cronus' sickle falling into the sea engendered Aphrodite (Venus to the Romans), the goddess of love; Uranus' blood falling on the land brought forth the nymphs, the giants, and also the Furies, who punish mortals who kill or injure their relatives.

Cronus, victorious, did not release the prisoners from Tartarus. He married his sister Rhea and set himself up as ruler of the world. To prevent Uranus' prophecy from coming true he swallowed all the children Rhea bore him; but when she bore Zeus she gave the child to Gaia to hide, and gave her husband a stone to swallow. Zeus was raised in secret. As he grew to maturity he asked the Titaness Metis to help him defeat his father and revive his siblings. Metis gave Cronus a potion that made him vomit forth his children, who promptly joined Zeus in making war on the Titans. After a ten-year struggle, Gaia urged Zeus to free the Cyclopes and Hecatoncheires, who would prove formidable allies; Zeus did so, and they armed him with the thunderbolt, also giving powerful weapons to his brother gods. Cronus and the other male Titans were then banished to Tartarus, promising that Zeus also would be overthrown by one of his sons. Atlas, who had led the Titans in war, was punished by being forced to hold up the world. Metis and the Titanesses remained free, as did the Titans Prometheus and Epimetheus, who had taken joined with the Olympians before the end.

The Olympian Gods (and a few others)

The Olympian gods, and the Titans who were left to rule with them, were the great supernatural figures in the foreground of the myths. However, they were not all-powerful. Their destinies as well as those of mortals were determined by the Moirae or Fates, three women who worked together on a tapestry whose threads were the lives of all living things. Their ancestry was unknown and their workings were mysterious, even to the gods.

Gods:

Zeus (called Jupiter or Jove by the Romans) was the greatest of the Olympian gods, ruler of the skies and wielder of the thunderbolt. His power was great but not infinite, and he could be deceived. He could also be deceitful--though married to Hera, he had frequent affairs with attractive goddesses, nymphs and mortal women, which he tried (usually unsuccessfully) to conceal from his wife. He expected righteous behavior from humans--oath-keeping, respect for the dead, and kindness to beggars and strangers.

Poseidon (Neptune to the Romans), brother of Zeus,was second greatest of the gods, the ruler of the sea, creator of horses, and wielder of an immensely powerful trident made for him by the Cyclopes.

Hades, (Pluto to the Romans), brother of Zeus, was the ruler of the underworld (named Hades after him) and the dead. He had a helmet of invisibility given to him by the Cyclopes.

Apollo, son of Zeus and the Titan Leto, twin brother of Artemis, was the god of the sun, the arts, and prophecy. He could not lie. His oracle at Delphi gave true answers to every question, although sometimes the truth was stated so mysteriously that the questioner went home no wiser. He also gave the gift of prophecy to Cassandra, a mortal woman, princess of Troy, when he was courting her; when she refused him, he couldn't take the gift back, but he added the curse that her prophecies would never be believed. Apollo was also the protector of herdsmen and shepherds and the father of Asclepius, the god of healing.

Dionysus (Bacchus to the Romans), son of Zeus and either Demeter or Semele depending on which myth you read, was the god of wine, fertility, ecstasy, madness, and the theater. His death and rebirth are associated with the changes of the seasons. He gave grapes to humans and taught the art of wine-making. Dionysus sometimes granted dangerous wishes to mortals. He offered King Midas anything he wanted, and Midas asked to have everything he touched turn to gold. Dionysus granted the wish and watched while the king's food and drink turned to gold as he touched them, while his dearly loved daughter went to comfort him and turned to gold as she embraced him. Then Dionysus had pity on the king, restored the girl to life and and took the gift back.

Eros (Cupid to the Romans) was the god of love and desire. In some stories he is one of the first gods to arise from chaos; in others he is the son of Aphrodite, by either her husband Hephaestus or her lover Ares. Eros' arrows, often shot at random, caused mortals and immortals who were struck by

8

them to fall in love. Eros himself fell in love with Psyche; their story is told below.

Ares (Mars to the Romans), son of Zeus and Hera, was the god of war in general (as opposed to defensive war, Athena's specialty). Many of the Greeks looked down on him as bloodthirsty and mindless; many of the Romans looked up to him as valiant and glorious.

Hermes (Mercury to the Romans), whose father was Zeus and whose mother was Atlas' daughter Maia, was the god of thieves and of commerce; as a day-old child he stole Apollo's cattle and, when Apollo came to reclaim them, got Apollo to leave them with him in exchange for the lyre, which he had just invented and was willing to trade away. Hermes also carried messages for Zeus and guided souls to the world of the dead. Pan, the god of shepherds, was Hermes' son.

Hephaestus (Vulcan to the Romans), son of Hera--some say hers only, some say hers by Zeus--was the smith to the gods, maker of their weapons and also of the lovely things which adorn Mount Olympus. He was crippled, having been thrown down from Olympus either by Hera (who was disappointed by his ugliness) or by Zeus (who was angry with him for standing up for his mother); but after his fall he was loved and honored by the Olympians. He was also honored by humans, to whom he taught metalwork and other necessary crafts. He was a gentle and peace-loving god. In many stories he was married to Aphrodite, though she was enamored of Ares and had an affair with him.

Prometheus was one of the Titans who survived into the age of the Olympian gods. In some stories he helped Athena to emerge from the head of Zeus. He was the maker and protector of humanity, at great cost to himself; he became the god of science. More of his story is told in "Prometheus, Epimetheus and Pandora" below.

Goddesses:

Hera, (Juno to the Romans), wife and sister of Zeus, was the protector of married women and mothers. Most of the stories about her describe her jealousy of Zeus and her revenges on his paramours.

Athena (Minerva to the Romans), who sprang full-fledged from the head of Zeus rather than being born in the usual way, was the goddess of wisdom and of defensive war (in most accounts--though in the Iliad she's described as being on the side of the Greek attackers of Troy.). Poseidon created horses, but Athena tamed them. She taught mortals to plow and raise crops and tame animals, she created the first olive tree, and she invented pottery, weaving and spinning. She could also be vindictive. When a mortal woman named Arachne claimed that she could weave as well as Athena, and actually challenged her to a weaving contest where she wove as skillfully as Athena (showing scenes of the Gods behaving foolishly, whereas Athena's tapestry showed the Gods in their glory), Athena destroyed Arachne's web and struck her with fear and shame so that she hanged herself. Athena pitied her then and brought her back to life as a spider. Our word 'arachnid' comes from Arachne's name.

Aphrodite (Venus to the Romans), born of the foam of the sea, was the goddess of love, supremely beautiful and the giver of joy. She could also be cruel, deceiving men and driving them to despair. In most myths her husband is Hephaestus and her lover is Ares.

Artemis (Diana to the Romans), daughter of Zeus and Leto and twin sister of Apollo, was the virgin goddess of the hunt, wilderness and wild creatures, virginity, childbirth and children. In later stories she is said to be the same as Selene, goddess of the moon, and Hecate, goddess of the underworld.

Demeter (Ceres to the Romans), sister of Zeus, was the goddess of the harvest and the earth's fertility. Athena taught men to plow, but Demeter gave them grain, and Demeter caused all growth. Demeter's beautiful daughter, **Persephone** (Proserpina to the Romans), was abducted by Hades; Demeter, who hadn't seen what happened, searched for her for a long time, grieving, and her grief stopped life and growth. Zeus, wishing the world to live, ordered Hades to send Persephone back; but Persephone had eaten in the Underworld and could not leave it forever. For four months of the year she was bound to return to Hades, and once again Demeter grieved and growth was halted, but for the remainder of the year Persephone was with her mother and all green things grew and thrived. According to some stories Dionysus is Demeter's son.

Hestia (Vesta to the Romans), sister of Zeus, was the virgin goddess of home and hearth.

Prometheus, Epimetheus and Pandora

Prometheus, whose name means Forethought, and his brother Epimetheus, whose name means Afterthought, were Titans, but before the end of the war between the Titans and the Olympians Prometheus had foreseen the victory of the Olympians and changed sides, persuading his brother to join him. After Zeus' victory when the rest of the Titans were imprisoned the brothers remained free and honored.

Prometheus was responsible for the making of humans. There are two different stories about how he did it.

In one account, Prometheus shaped the bodies of the first men from clay, and he called on Athene to give them living souls. Once they lived he taught them mathematics, science and all manner of wisdom. He also taught them about the gods, and they saw the necessity of making sacrifices to beings so much more powerful to themselves. Indeed this was wise, since the gods were taking notice of these new creatures and were inclined to be jealous of their growing powers. Zeus suggested destroying them, but Prometheus defended them and they were spared. When a question arose as to which parts of a sacrificed animal had to be actually given to the gods. Prometheus urged men to let the gods choose, but he himself divided the sacrifice in question, hiding the good meat in one pile under dirt and organs, and hiding the bones and skin under a layer of gleaming fat. Zeus chose the second pile without looking beneath the top layer. When he realized what he'd chosen Zeus was furious, but he couldn't take his choice back. Instead he withheld the gift of fire from men, saying they could eat their meat raw. Prometheus asked Athene to let him into Olympus secretly, which she did. There he stole fire from the sun, brought it down to men and showed them its uses.

In another creation story Prometheus and his brother Epimetheus were tasked with assigning gifts to all the living creatures. Epimetheus set to work in haste, giving out strong wings, sharp teeth and claws, warm fur, night vision, strength, speed and endurance to all the beasts. He had quite run out of gifts when he came to men, who were left naked and defenseless. Prometheus pitied them, raised them to stand upright and made them in the image of the gods, stole fire for them and taught them to use it.

Prometheus realized that Zeus was likely to be angry with him, with Epimetheus, and with men. He urged Epimetheus never to accept any gift from Zeus. Epimetheus agreed, but he forgot.

Later Zeus came to Epimetheus and offered him a great gift--a woman perfect in grace and beauty, named Pandora, the all-gifted. Some stories say that Epimetheus married her at once with joy. Others say that he remembered her brother's warning and refused her at first, but after he saw how Zeus punished Prometheus for his defiance Epimetheus decided that it was wiser not to defy him, and he married her. In either case, on Pandora's wedding day the gods gave her a gift as well--a beautiful box which they told her she must never open. Pandora agreed, but day by day her curiosity grew more intense, and at last she opened the box--just a crack, just to take a quick look. At once the plagues of mankind which the gods had hidden in the box flew out: sickness, old age, madness, grief and more. The last thing left in the box was the one beautiful one: Hope, who gave men strength to bear all the other evils and keep living and striving--although poets have disagreed from that day to this about whether this persistence is a blessing or a curse.

Zeus knew that Prometheus would not be easily deceived, so he took revenge on him by main force. He had Prometheus bound in unbreakable chains to a mountain peak, where he hung in pain, exposed to the taunts of his enemies and the ineffectual pity of his friends. Prometheus didn't repent of what he had done for men. He did voice his regret at having supported Zeus, who had shown himself to be so ungrateful, and he solaced himself by reflecting that Zeus also would be overthrown in the end, and that he, Prometheus, was the only one who knew who was to supplant Zeus, therefore the only one who could avert Zeus's doom. Zeus, hearing this, sent Hermes to demand a thorough explanation of this threat. Prometheus refused to answer any questions unless he was set free. Hermes replied that Zeus didn't need to bargain with him and would make him suffer even more if he remained defiant. Prometheus didn't yield. Zeus then sent an eagle to tear Prometheus' flesh and devour his liver, and caused his body to renew itself every day only to suffer the same agony again. Prometheus continued to declare that he was righteous and Zeus a despot, and he gave no information; in bitter pride and desperate courage he endured his pain for many generations of men, until Hercules was born, grew to his full strength and destroyed the eagle.

Psyche and Eros

Psyche was a mortal king's daughter so beautiful that some of her father's subjects neglected to praise and worship Aphrodite and brought their gifts and their songs of praise to Psyche instead. Aphrodite was furious and planned revenge. She ordered her son Eros to shoot Psyche with one of his arrows of desire and cause her to fall in love with some ugly brute. Some tales say that Eros accidentally pierced his own skin with the arrow-point, others that he simply took a good look at Psyche and fell in love with her himself. In any case, he didn't do what Aphrodite ordered. Indeed, Psyche did not fall in love at all, and no one asked for her hand in marriage, though her less beautiful older sisters were soon royally wed. Her parents, dismayed, asked Apollo's oracle how they could find their daughter a husband. The oracle told them to take her to a deserted place and leave her there to be found by the winged serpent, terrifying even to the gods, who had chosen her for his own. Her parents were distressed but didn't dare to disobey the god. Psyche did not join in the general lamentation. She said that the end would come soon and she was well enough. She kept her courage up even as they left her in the wilderness alone at nightfall.

But it was Eros who came to her in the darkness, having begged Apollo's help. He took her to his beautiful castle. By day she was alone there; by night her husband came to her, always in darkness, telling her that she must never strike a light while he was there or try to look at him.

Psyche was lonely by day and missed her sisters. When

they were brought to the castle they were jealous of its splendor. They asked Psyche about her husband. She said that he was loving and gentle and good, and that he was away from home just then; she stammered and contradicted herself when they asked how he looked. The sisters said that they could tell she'd never seen him, and that only something foul would hide itself in darkness. The gods, they said, had assured them that he was a monster and would kill Psyche if she did not kill him first. They urged her over and over to look at him, see him for the beast he was, and destroy him.

Psyche did not wish to kill her husband, but she did desperately want to see him. That night after he slept she lit the lamp and stared in amazement at his beauty. As she stared she let hot oil from the lamp fall on his shoulder. He woke in pain, saw that he had been disobeyed, and fled, leaving Psyche alone.

Psyche made long and desperate journeys seeking her husband and did not find him. At last, despairing, she sought out Aphrodite, who was tending Eros while he recovered from his burn. Aphrodite mocked her and then set her a series of impossible tasks. First she set Psyche before a great mound of tiny seeds of several kinds, ordering her to sort them out before nightfall on pain of dire but unspecified punishment. But the ants pitied Psyche and did that task for her. Then Aphrodite ordered her to gather some of the precious wool from the ferocious sheep who bore golden fleece. A reed by the river told Psyche to leave the sheep alone and gather the wool which was caught on the briars by the water where they went to drink. Then Aphrodite ordered her to bring a pitcher of water from the source of the river Styx, which could only be reached by climbing down a steep and slimy cliff. An eagle saw Psyche preparing to climb down, took her pitcher and brought her the water. At last Aphrodite, growing desperate, sent Psyche to the Underworld itself to ask Persephone for some of her beauty in a box. Psyche went. She paid the ferryman over the river of death a coin so that he would bring her back again; she gave a sweet cake to the terrible three-headed hound who guarded the castle of Hades, and he ate it and let her pass. She hurried back with the box, but before entering Aphrodite's house she couldn't resist opening the box to look inside. Straightaway she fell into a sleep like death.

Eros, however, was healed. Ignoring his mother's insistence that he needed more rest, he slipped out the window (she having locked his door) and saw Psyche on the ground beside the box from the Underworld. He revived her and brought her to Zeus, who made her immortal and gave his blessing to their marriage. Aphrodite, after that, was too prudent to object.

Oedipus and His Children

I: Self-Fulfilling Prophecies

King Laius of Thebes and his wife Jocasta were warned by Apollo's oracle at Delphi that their son would kill his father. Laius knew that the oracle never lied, but he still hoped to change his fate. He bound his infant son's feet together and gave him to a shepherd, ordering the man to abandon the baby in the wilderness, hoping in this way to avoid direct blood guilt and also to prevent the boy from growing up to kill him.

But the shepherd, instead of abandoning the child, gave him to another shepherd who lived outside Theban territory. The second shepherd brought the child to his own king, Polybus of Corinth, who had long been childless. Polybus named the child Oedipus and raised him as his own.

Oedipus grew up loving his adopted parents and believing he had been born to them. Once when he was a young man a drunk told him that he was not in fact his father's son. Oedipus was distressed and went to the oracle at Delphi to ask about his parentage. The oracle didn't tell him who his true parents were, but it did tell him that he would kill his father and marry his mother. Horrified, Oedipus fled the country, vowing never to see his parents again lest he should do them harm.

On his flight, at a place where three highways met, Oedipus met an old man in a carriage, attended by four servants. That man ordered Oedipus roughly to get out of the road and out of the way of his betters. The carriage-driver shoved Oedipus aside; Oedipus, offended, struck the driver. The old man in the carriage hit Oedipus across the head with his heavy goad. Oedipus hit him back so hard that he was thrown from the carriage, dead. Oedipus also killed three of the old man's attendants. One only escaped to bring word back to the city.

As he continued his journey Oedipus heard rumors of the evil fate that had befallen the city of Thebes. The Sphinx, a monstrous lion with wings and a woman's face, had stationed herself outside the city gate. She seized every traveler who left the city, promising to let him go if he answered her riddle. None answered rightly; all were killed. Thebes was under siege, its citizens hungry and desperate.

Oedipus was less afraid of dying than of living to fulfill Apollo's prophecy. He set out to meet the Sphinx, and he answered her riddle rightly. Thwarted of her prey, she killed herself, and the road to Thebes was safe again. The grateful Thebans made Oedipus king, since their own king, Laius, was dead--killed by robbers, so rumors said, as he went to seek help from the oracle. Oedipus married the royal widow, Jocasta, who bore him two sons and two daughters. Oedipus was loved by his wife and by his people.

But a plague fell on Thebes. The crops were blighted in the ground, pregnant women miscarried in great pain, and sickness spread rapidly in all parts of the city. Oedipus sent Jocasta's brother Creon to the oracle to ask what he could do to save Thebes. This time the oracle answered the question directly. The plague, it said, would be lifted once the Thebans had avenged King Laius by killing or banishing the man who had killed him. Oedipus asked the people why this had not been done already, and they explained that the fear of the Sphinx had driven other matters from their minds. Oedipus pronounced curses on Laius' killer and also on anyone who sheltered the killer, and then started making inquiries.

First he sent for the blind prophet Teiresias, who came unwillingly and initially refused to give answers. Oedipus begged him to speak for the city's sake and then accused Teiresias of having plotted the murder. Teiresias indignantly denied the accusation and told Oedipus that he himself was the murderer. Oedipus called the prophet a liar, a hireling paid by Creon to discredit Oedipus and give Creon the throne. He sent Teiresias away, called Creon and threatened to kill him as a traitor. But Jocasta pled with him to spare Creon's life and believe that the prophet spoke in his own malice, not at Creon's prompting. She knew, she said, how prophecies could lie. Why, it had been prophesied that her first husband, Laius, should be killed by his own son, but instead he was struck down by strangers at a place where three roads met.

Oedipus was alarmed, not reassured. He asked what Laius had looked like and who had traveled with him. The description matched that of the group which had shoved him out of the way years before. Oedipus sent for the servant who had survived the attack on Laius, still hoping that that man would report Laius killed by a robber band in agreement with the rumor, not by a solitary man. While Oedipus was still struggling with his fears a messenger came from Corinth to report the death of King Polybus. Oedipus gave thanks that at least he had been preserved from his curse--that his father had died, not by his hand, and that his flight from Corinth had not been in vain. The messenger told him that he had no need to flee Corinth--that Polybus had only fostered him, not sired him. Oedipus asked how the messenger could know that. The messenger revealed himself as the shepherd who had received Oedipus as a castaway child from a Theban shepherd and delivered him to Polybus.

Just then the Theban who had seen Laius' death arrived, and the Corinthian messenger recognized and greeted him as the fellow-shepherd who had brought him the child. The Theban muttered to the Corinthian to say no more. Oedipus threatened him with torture if he didn't tell all he knew. The Theban, terrified, admitted that he had received the child from Queen Jocasta, who ordered him to leave the child to die lest he should kill his father Laius.

Oedipus, horrified, recognized that both he and Laius had brought their curses to fruition by trying to avoid them. Jocasta killed herself in her shame. Oedipus blinded himself and begged the Thebans to kill him, thus saving themselves from the curse and him from a miserable life, but Creon refused this plea at first, keeping Oedipus in the royal palace.

II: Curses and Blessings

As time passed Oedipus' shame grew less bitter, and he reflected that he had sinned through no fault of his own--for he counted parricide and incest as faults but seems to have thought an ungovernable temper was a fitting quality in a king. He stopped asking to die or to leave Thebes, which was now plague-free. Creon then decided to banish him. Oedipus' sons, Polyneices and Eteocles, chose to stay in the city, which they both wished to rule, and they did not protest their father's banishment, perhaps seeing him as either a rival or an embarrassment. Oedipus' daughters were more concerned for their father. Antigone shared his exile, leading him by the hand and begging for food and shelter for both of them. They got little enough; people were reluctant to share either in Oedipus' guilt or in his misfortune. Ismene went back and forth as a messenger, bringing her father news from Thebes.

After many years of wandering Oedipus claimed refuge at the holy place of Colonus, outside Athens. The elders of Colonus tried to turn him away at first, but he managed to persuade them that he had done no evil willingly. They called on Theseus, king of Athens, who had compassion on Oedipus and agreed to give him shelter and protection, either in the city itself or in the holy place. Oedipus chose the latter.

Ismene came to her father at Colonus bearing bad news. Oedipus' sons had fought over who would rule Thebes. The younger son, Eteocles, had gained the favor of Creon and the people and ruled along with Creon; the older, Polyneices, was raising a band of warriors to attack Thebes and install himself as king. Both sons, Ismene warned, would soon be coming to seek their father, for Apollo's oracle had predicted safety, prosperity and victory for the city where Oedipus died and was buried.

Creon arrived hard on her heels, expressing great pity for Oedipus and promising to bring him back to his native land. Oedipus answered bitterly, blaming Creon for exiling him in the first place and accusing him of feigning pity in order to secure Apollo's blessing. Creon responded by seizing Antigone and Ismene, sending them away under guard, repeating the ugly tale of Oedipus's deeds and urging the elders of Colonus not to take Oedipus in, given the curse he bore. The elders replied that they knew the story and had chosen to welcome Oedipus. Creon then threatened to take Oedipus away by force and keep him imprisoned until he learned to repent of his insolence. The elders, however, had sent for Theseus, who arrived in time to stop Creon laying hands on Oedipus. Theseus' soldiers recaptured Antigone and Ismene and restored them to Oedipus, who cursed Creon and sent him away with only a father's curse to bring to Eteocles.

Polyneices came soon after, professing remorse at having allowed his father to be banished; he himself had felt the bitterness of poverty and exile, he said, and repented that he had condemned his father to the same fate. He urged his father to come with the band attacking Thebes. Oedipus trusted his motives no more than Creon's, asked the gods to grant that Polyneices and Eteocles might kill each other, and sent his son away. Antigone begged her brother not to go to war against Thebes, but he refused to listen, saying that he couldn't fight his fate, and adding that he was afraid of being thought a coward. While he wouldn't take his sister's advice, he asked her to bury him if he was killed in the battle for Thebes.

Oedipus, estranged from his sons and grateful for Theseus' protection, died and was buried outside Athens, leaving his blessing on that city. Antigone and Ismene, valuing family ties more than prudence, went home to Thebes.

III. Conflicting Duties

In Thebes the battle between Polyneices' forces and Eteocles' was long and bitter, but Creon and the Thebans won, although Eteocles died in killing his brother. Creon gave Eteocles a hero's funeral, but he commanded that Polyneices and the others who had fallen attacking the city should be left unburied for the dogs and the birds to eat. He set guards over the corpses and vowed to kill anyone who mourned for or tried to bury men who had committed what he saw as the gravest possible crime, treason.

Antigone, though she was betrothed to Creon's son Haemon, abhorred the order, knowing that the souls of the unburied dead were condemned to wander homeless throughout eternity as her father had done in life. She urged Ismene to help her bury Polyneices. Ismene protested that they had no chance and their family had already suffered enough from stubborn pride. Antigone urged their duty toward the dead and the gods, but Ismene would not be persuaded to help, although she promised not to tell Creon what her sister planned.

Soon after the guards came to Creon in distress, reporting that someone had covered Polyneices with dirt in the dark of night and gone away undetected. Creon accused the guards of taking bribes and threatened them with torture if they didn't bring the guilty party in. The gods unburied the body and sat down to wait. A dust storm blinded them for a little while, but when the dust cleared there was Antigone, pouring funeral drink offerings at the feet of her brother, whom she had managed to shallowly bury again. The guards pitied Antigone, but they pitied themselves more, and they seized her and brought her before Creon.

Creon, outraged, accused her of willfully breaking the law and destroying civil order. Antigone, equally outraged, accused him of willfully breaking the divine law which required protection of the dead and kindness to relatives. Creon argued that in showing kindness to Polyneices Antigone acted as an enemy to Eteocles. She replied that it was in her nature to join in loving, not in hating. "Pass then to the world of the dead," Creon told her, "and, if thou must needs love, love them." He tried to have Ismene condemned as well, having seen her raving and weeping in the house. Ismene claimed that she had shared in her sister's crime, but Antigone would have none of it, and the Thebans believed Antigone.

Haemon heard the news and arrived in time to ask his father to spare Antigone's life, but Creon would not listen. Haemon left in a rage of grief, and Creon had Polyneices unburied again and Antigone sealed into a cave to starve. The Thebans wept for her but were too prudent to intervene--all but the prophet Teiresias, who heard of Antigone's fate, hurried to Creon and told him that his actions were hateful to the gods. Creon, like Oedipus before him, accused Teiresias of having been hired to undermine him. Teiresias denied the accusation, repeated his warning, and added that if Creon did not make haste to bury Polyneices and save Antigone, Creon would suffer the loss of his own son.

The city elders urged Creon to heed the warning, and eventually he gave in, first burying what was left of Polyneices with all proper solemnities and then going to release Antigone. He came too late, as Haemon his son had done before him. Antigone had killed herself instead of waiting to starve; Haemon in his furious grief killed himself to join her; and when she heard the news Eurydice, Creon's wife, also took her own life, cursing her husband. Creon, bereft of his family, found little consolation in his patriotism.

Creon did not learn from his mistakes. He was still King of Thebes, and he still refused burial to Polyneices' companions. The families of the dead men came to Theseus at Athens and begged him to march against Thebes and compel Creon to bury their families. Theseus let the Athenians vote on the matter, and they agreed to the campaign. First Theseus pled with Creon to grant the burial rites and have peace, but Creon in his bitter pride refused. The Athenians then attacked and won, and the Thebans expected the sack of their city and the slaughter of their citizens. Theseus, however, restrained his army. They had come to bury the dead and honor the gods, he said, not to cause further destruction. After giving the dead a splendid though belated funeral the army went home again to Athens.

The young sons of the dead men, however, were less merciful. Ten years later they attacked Thebes seeking vengeance for their fathers. They destroyed the city completely.

The Trojan War

I. Jealousies

The Trojan war, it is said, had its origin in the jealousies of the Olympians, though it was mortals who suffered and died in it. Eris, the goddess of discord, started an argument among the goddesses about which of them was the most beautiful. Zeus, refusing to comment on the matter, sent the three leading candidates--Hera, Aphrodite and Athena--to a mortal, Paris, nephew of the King of Troy, urging them to let him judge.

Each goddess offered the judge a substantial bribe. Hera offered to make him sovereign over Europe and Asia. Athena (not yet settled into her role supporting law and defense) offered to lead him to a decisive victory over the Greeks. Aphrodite promised to give him the most beautiful woman in the world. Paris accepted Aphrodite's offer.

Aphrodite made good on her promise; the only problem was that the unmatched mortal beauty, Helen, was already married to another man--to Menelaus, whose brother was Agamemnon of Argos, richest and most powerful of the kings of Greece. Furthermore, Helen's father, fearing that her beauty would lead to war, had made all the kings who sought her hand promise that, once she was married, they would avenge themselves on anyone who tried to take her from her husband. Paris didn't let that stop him. He came to Menelaus' house as a guest, won his trust and then eloped with his wife, betraying the sacred law of hospitality. Menelaus called on his brother for help, and Agamemnon called all the other rulers who had courted Helen--in fact, nearly all the rulers of Greece-- to join him in attacking Troy, punishing Paris, and bringing Helen back.

II. Battles and Betrayals

A huge army gathered and prepared to set sail for Troy, but the winds were against them; day after day, week after week, the army waited va inly for navigable weather. At last a prophet announced that the winds were caused by the displeasure of Artemis. One of the Greeks--not named--had killed a hare, one of the animals sacred to her, together with its young; in return, she demanded the death of Iphigenia, the eldest daughter of the war-host's leader, Agamemnon.

Agamemnon was appalled, but his pride was stronger than his family feeling. He sent a message to his wife Clytemnestra, telling her to come with Iphigenia so that Iphigenia could be married to Achilles. When his daughter arrived he had her killed on Artemis' altar. The winds turned in their favor, and the Greek fleet sailed to Troy. Clytemnestra returned to Argos, mourned for her daughter and planned revenge.

The war dragged on for nine years, and the sides were evenly matched. The Greeks had Achilles, mightiest of all warriors; the Trojans had Hector, noblest and best of men, second only to Achilles in prowess; both armies had huge numbers of determined men. Both, also, had some help from the Olympians. Aphrodite, Ares, Artemis and Apollo supported the Trojans, while Athena, Hera and Poseidon favored the Greeks; all changed the course of the war at different points by magically wounding the leaders of their enemies or snatching their wounded favorites out of danger.

While the Greeks were unable to break into the city of Troy itself, they did a certain amount of plundering in the surrounding lands, and on one of these expeditions Agamemnon abducted Chryseis, a beautiful girl whose father was a priest of Apollo. Apollo resented this and struck the Greek army with sickness. It was Achilles who finally gathered the Greeks together and urged them to do whatever was needed to pacify Apollo. Agamemnon was finally forced, resentfully, to surrender Chryseis to her father. In revenge, however, he took for himself Achilles' war-captured concubine, Briseis. Achilles refused to take any further part in the battle against Troy; why, he asked, should he help one woman-stealer to avenge himself on another? He stayed in his own camp with his friend and lover Patroclus. Agamemnon pressed on the attack without Achilles and was repulsed with great losses; the Greeks were driven back to the ships in which they'd sailed to Troy. One of those ships was fired; it seemed clear that the rest must follow and the Greeks would be slaughtered.

Patroclus was distressed and begged to borrow Achilles' armor. Achilles agreed reluctantly, telling him to be careful, not to get too far into the forefront of the battle, not to push the attack too far toward Troy. For Patroclus, while brave, was not as powerful a fighter as Achilles. Some stories say that when Achilles was an infant his mother, the sea-nymph Thetis, had dipped him in the holy river Styx to make him invulnerable to mortal wounds; however, in the dipping process she held him by his heel, which therefore remained unprotected. Patroclus had no such protection.

When a figure in Achilles' armor joined the combat, the Trojans were alarmed and began to fall back, while the Greeks took courage and drove their enemies back to the walls of Troy. The disguised Patroclus led them on, forgetting all Achilles' warnings until Hector, the champion of Troy, attacked him directly. Then it became all too clear that Patroclus lacked Achilles' strength. Hector killed him, and his helmet fell away and showed both armies that Achilles had never taken part in that battle.

Achilles was told of Patroclus' death, and he reproached himself bitterly for letting his wounded pride keep him from protecting his people and his friend. He told the Greeks that he had done wrong, and he promised to lead them the next day. That night his mother Thetis came to him, bringing magical arms and armor made by Hephaestus, the smith of the gods.

Lead them he did, and the gods fought each other on Olympus while the mortals fought on earth. But Achilles was invincible, and the Greeks followed him in fury, and the Trojans fell back to their walls. Most of the Trojan army retreated into the city; Hector only, desperate to save his family and the other noncombatants within the walls, stood before the gates and offered to fight alone against Achilles. He asked first that Achilles should agree that the loser would be buried with honor. Achilles refused that request. If he and Hector had fought unaided Hector might have had the victory, but Athena strengthened Achilles' arms and weakened Hector, who died knowing who was against him and fighting without hope.

Achilles, still furious over Patroclus' death, dragged Hector's body round the walls of Troy and then vowed to leave it unburied for the dogs; but Hector's aged father, Priam the King of Troy, came himself to Achilles, unarmed, and begged for his son's body. Achilles repented then, seeing Priam's grief, and there was a truce while the Trojans buried and mourned for Hector, whom they had loved for his gentleness as much as his strength.

31

III. Lies

Hector's death and their own peril hardened the resolve of the Trojans, and after the truce ended they fought more fiercely than before. And the Greeks also lost their champion Achilles; Paris, Helen's lover, hid in ambush and shot him in the heel, and he died. It seemed that neither side could conquer finally by force of arms. Odysseus, cleverest of the Greek leaders, thought of another approach.

One morning the Trojans awoke to see with amazement that the Greek army was gone, the ships nowhere to be seen. All that was left before the walls of Troy was a vast wooden statue in the shape of a horse. Cassandra the prophetess warned that the horse was a danger to them and must be destroyed, but no one believed her. Going into what had been the Greek camp, the Trojans found only one person there, a terrified man who begged for his life and said he never wanted to be a Greek again. The Greeks, he said, had been daunted by the strength of Troy and realized that the gods were fighting against them. They wanted to return home, but once again the winds were against them, and once again the prophet told them that only a human sacrifice would allow them safe passage over the seas. The captured Greek said that he had been chosen as the sacrifice; he had managed to escape, and the Greeks had sailed without him, and now he hated them and asked their foes for mercy. The Trojans pitied him and agreed to take him in. But what, they asked, was the wooden horse? An offering to the gods, their captive said. The Greeks had hoped that the Trojans would destroy the horse and incur the wrath of the gods, and feared that they would take it into the city and so bring down the gods' blessing on themselves.

So the Trojan horse was brought inside the city walls with great rejoicing, and that night the people of Troy lay down to sleep in peace for the first time in many years. Meanwhile the Greek warriors who had hidden themselves inside the horse opened a hidden trapdoor and climbed out to open the city gates to the rest of the Greek army, which had sailed away only far enough to be hidden from the city, and had returned under cover of darkness. Soon Troy was burning; most of its people woke too late to fight effectively, and the rest were hopelessly outnumbered. By morning the last resistance had been broken, Hector's old father and his infant son were killed, and all the people of Troy were dead or bound for a life of slavery in Greece.

IV. Homecomings

It may be that the brutal sacking of Troy displeased the gods. On the voyage back from Troy a terrible storm struck the Greek fleet, widely scattering the ships. Odysseus' vessel was blown into uncharted seas, and he had to make a long and terrible voyage, overcoming monsters, maelstroms, and beautiful but deadly illusions, before he could return his wife, Penelope, who waited patiently for him and cleverly kept her increasingly greedy suitors at bay. The story of that voyage, narrated in Homer's Odyssey, is too long to tell properly here. Other Greek leaders had less celebrated but similarly harrowing journeys.

Agamemnon had an easier voyage, arriving safely in the port of Argos, where his subjects cheered him as the conqueror of Troy and did him great honor. In public all praised him. In private some of them murmured to each other, remembering how they had seen Iphigenia and Clytemnestra sail away gladly to what they thought would be a wedding, how Clytemnestra had come home without her daughter and with a darkness behind her eyes. They knew that Clytemnestra had taken a lover, Aegisthus, whose father had an old grievance against Agamemnon's father, and they knew that Clytemnestra had not dismissed him upon hearing that her husband was coming home.

Agamemnon heard only the laudatory speeches, the cheering, and the music of the festival procession that escorted him home. When he reached his palace Clytemnestra welcomed him effusively, and they went inside together.

Soon after the crowd heard a man's voice crying out in agony from within the palace. The doors opened and Clytemnestra stood framed in them, bloodstained and proud, declaring that she had killed Agamemnon and avenged Iphigenia, and that from then on she and her lover would rule all things well.

Clytemnestra and Aegisthus would have killed Agamemnon's son, Orestes, lest he should grow up disposed to avenge his father's murder, but the boy's sister Electra hurried him out of the house in secret and sent him away with their elderly tutor into a hidden exile. Electra and her younger sister Chrysothemis remained in the palace in Argos. No one feared them. Chrysothemis, who acted as a dutiful daughter to her mother, seems to have had a fairly comfortable life, although she was not permitted to marry lest her husband should take up the blood-feud for Agamemnon.

Electra was another matter. She had adored her father, and she praised and mourned him fiercely, publicly and perpetually, year after year after year. She called her mother and stepfather murderers just as plainly and openly. In private she sent messages to Orestes in exile, reminding him of the duty he owed to his heroic father, and lamenting the bitterness of her own life. Clytemnestra and Aegisthus did not kill her-- perhaps Clytemnestra had a fondness for all her daughters, not Iphigenia only, or perhaps she thought a girl could do her no harm. But Electra was treated with contempt and asked to do work which she considered beneath her father's daughter. She did the work, but she refused to bridle her tongue. At last Clytemnestra and Aegisthus, wearied by her bitter speeches-- and also, perhaps, afraid of Orestes, who was no longer a boy but a young man--began to speak of having her imprisoned where she couldn't incite anyone else to assail them.

That plan became unnecessary, as they thought, when a messenger came to tell the royal family that Orestes, still in foreign parts, had died in a chariot race. Electra despaired, but

Clytemnestra laughed and praised the gods who had kept her safe.

Electra fled to her father's grave to mourn all her dead. The messenger followed her there and revealed himself to her as Orestes, come for vengeance. Electra was fiercely joyful. Orestes was not. He knew that it was a horrible crime before the gods to fail to avenge a parent, and an equally horrible crime to kill one, and he saw no other alternative. He had gone to the oracle at Delphi and been told that his first duty was to avenge his father. He had come to obey the oracle, but he hated the thought of it.

His hatred did not stop him. Returning to the castle, he was welcomed by the royal pair, who learned their error only minutes before they died.

Orestes came back out, bloodied and stumbling. Electra came to praise and comfort him, but he hardly heard her. The people outside the gates argued over whether he deserved to be crowned as his father's heir and avenger or stoned to death as a mother-murderer. He didn't heed them. He stared at something no one else could see. They knew, though, what he must be seeing: the Erinyes, the Furies, the avengers of blood. These goddesses older than the Olympians, daughters of Darkness, snaky-haired and iron-hooved, pursued and tormented those who killed relatives--though it seems they had left Agamemnon alone. They had no such mercy on Orestes. Wild-eyed and guilt-ridden, he fled the town.

V. Mercies

Apollo, however, had not forgotten that Orestes had acted in obedience to the Delphic oracle. When Orestes drew near Delphi again in his wanderings Apollo in his own shrine was able to lull the Furies to sleep long enough to offer Orestes the ritual cleansing for blood guilt. That wasn't enough to free him from the Furies, but it was enough to entitle Orestes to plead his case before the gods. That trial, however, could not take place at Delphi; Apollo was too closely involved in it to be its judge. He told Orestes to go on to Athens and submit himself to Athena's judgment. Orestes just had time to undergo the ritual, hear the advice and flee again before the Furies awoke and pursued him.

Finally Orestes arrived in Athens. Ragged, barefoot, bleeding and frenzied, he staggered into Athene's holy place, clasped the feet of her statue and asked her to decide his case once and for all. He owned that he had done a horrible thing, for which all that he had suffered might be a just punishment; he also said that he had thought it less horrible than the alternative. He was weary of not knowing, and he asked her to judge straightaway so that he might die and be cast into Tartarus or else live with a sound mind.

Apollo and the Furies, who had both followed Orestes closely, immediately began to plead their cases for and against him. Athena, reluctant to interfere in a divine quarrel, called in the men of Athens to hear the case and cast their votes; so the last terrible aftershock of the Trojan War ended, as the incident that started the war had begun, with mortals judging between gods.

The Furies described the full horror of matricide and urged that, if Orestes was pardoned for so grave a sin, no parents would thereafter be safe from their children. They also hinted heavily that if Orestes, their lawful prey, was taken from them, they could find ways of venting their malice on Athens. Apollo described the horror of killing a husband and argued that, if Orestes was condemned for avenging so grave a sin, no husbands would thereafter be safe from their wives. He also argued that children owed more to fathers than mothers, since the germ of life came from the man and the woman simply harbored it until birth (this was considered good science at the time), and reminded the hearers that he also was a God powerful to reward and punish.

The Athenians weighed the arguments, and the threats also, and their votes were evenly divided. Athena, agreeing with Apollo's case for the greater value of paternity and also pitying Orestes' long anguish, cast a tie-breaking vote to hold Orestes innocent and keep the Furies from him ever after. The Furies denounced Athena, Athens, and the disrespect which both Olympians and mortals showed to their ancient race, and they threatened the city with plagues, madness and sterility. Athena urged them to reconsider, flattered their age and wisdom, and promised that they would always be honored and revered in Athens if only they would change their curses to blessings and protect both the city and those suppliants who might seek it out in the future. The Furies were persuaded, and after that time they were worshipped as the Eumenides, the Mercies. And it seems that their mercy rested on Orestes and Electra. Both married and had children, but the stories do not suggest that these children were tainted with the family's curse.

The Minotaur

I. Minos and Poseidon

The story of the Minotaur started on the island of Crete. It began when the King of Crete, Asterion died. The King had three step sons from his wife Europa. It was said that the three were actually the sons of Zeus who had seduced Europa. The god of the Skies had taken on the form of a bull and as a result of their union, Europa bore three sons, Sarpedon, Rhadamanthus and Minos.

All three princes were well-loved by Asterion. So it had not been made clear which of the three would succeed him. Each prince had his own argument as to why he should be crowned as the next ruler of Crete. But it was Minos who had the most convincing and powerful claim.

Minos, whose name in Cretan literally meant king, boasted that he had the gods' favor. He claimed that out of the three brothers, he was the one that the Olympians wanted to rule over Crete. The gods would grant him anything he prayed for and this was the reason he should be crowned King.

To prove his claim and to secure the throne, he prayed to Poseidon and asked for a bull to be sent from the sea. He pledged that this animal would be sacrificed back to Poseidon to show Minos' dedication and loyalty to the Olympians.

And right before everybody's eyes, a magnificent white bull

rose from the sea and walked onto the shore. So majestic was the creature that there was no doubt that it came from Poseidon. This was the proof that everyone needed to confirm that Minos was the rightful heir to the throne. Once crowned, he sent his two brothers away from Crete and banished them out of the land.

It would've been the perfect ending to the story had Minos not become too greedy. Despite already being King of Crete, Minos wanted more. He wanted to keep the bull that had risen from the sea. He felt that as the ruler, it was his right to have such a magnificent beast. So instead of sacrificing it to Poseidon as he had promised, he chose one of the bulls from his own heard. While the bull he had chosen could've been a worthy sacrifice, it was not what he had promised.

Now if there was anything that the gods don't like it was broken promises. Poseidon was enraged by Minos' treachery so he decided to teach the new king a lesson. The curse that he sent was befitting Minos' offense.

II. Poseidon's Punishment

Poseidon made Pasiphae, Minos' wife, fall in love with the bull he sent to be a sacrifice. So great was the Queen's passion for the beast that she lusted after it. She had Daedalus create a wooden cow covered in cowhide. She then had this brought to the field where the bull grazed.

Pasiphae climbed inside Daedalus' creation and waited for the bull to approach. And sure enough she caught the attention of her heart's desire. The bull saw the wooden cow and was besotted. This was how Pasiphae was able to consummate her lust for the beast. The Queen became pregnant after this mating.

Poseidon's punishment was ironic and just. The bull that Minos had kept instead of sacrificing had impregnated his wife and the creature that was born from the union was a constant reminder of what the King of Crete had done.

There are some versions of the myth though that tell a different story. While Poseidon may have been saddened and angered by Minos's hubris, some say that it was actually Aphrodite who had cursed the poor Queen.

Pasiphae, according to this other version, had neglected to show piety, which caught Aphrodite's wrath. The Queen after all was by no means a mere mortal. Pasiphae was the daughter of the sun god Helios and the Oceanid Perse. The Queen's arrogance, as well as her husband's betrayal, were the reasons the goddess of beauty cursed her with her insatiable desire for the bull.

But whether it was Poseidon or Aphrodite that had caused this wild passion, it was the result that merits mention.

Pasiphae gave birth to a child that was half human and half bull. It had the body of a man but a hideous head of a bull. Since it was an unnatural creature, its diet, as well, was neither that of a human nor that of a bull. The creature fed on human flesh. This child was named Asterion but became better known as the Minotaur.

Minos was furious when he found out what happened. Asterion's appearance was a constant reminder of his wife's infidelity and affair with the beast. He also found out that Daedalus and his wife Icarus had been responsible for building the wooden cow that Pasiphae had used to mate with the bull. He enslaved the father and son and sought out the help of the Oracle at Delphi.

The Oracle told Minos that the best way to hide the Minotaur was to keep it in a Labyrinth. So the King commanded Daedalus and his son to build the Labyrinth beneath the palace. Once this was completed, the Minotaur was left to roam it, away from the Kingdom's people.

Minos was said to throw his enemies into the Labyrinth to feed the monstrous half man and half bull and it would seem like this would be a perfect ending but Minos would put the Minotaur to more use.

III. The Tribute of the Seven Youths and Seven Maidens

While the labyrinth was being built, Minos' only son with Pasiphae, Androgeos was killed. There are different stories told about the death of the young prince. In one story, it was said that the Athenians were jealous of Androgeos constantly winning the Panathenic games. And to show their displeasure they killed the Prince.

Another story tells that it was Aegeus, the King of Athens that had caused the death of Androgeos. The King had been angered at the Prince's victories in the Panathenic games, so he sent the younger man to slay the Marathonian Bull. It was the same bull that Androgeos mother Pasiphae had fallen in love with. It was also the same bull that had gotten the Queen pregnant with the Minotaur.

Whichever story one chooses to believe, what was clear was that it was the Athenians that Minos blamed for the death of his son. He demanded retribution for the loss of the young Prince. His demand was for Athens to send 7 youths and 7 maidens to be sent every year to Crete. These tributes would be fed to the Minotaur.

The Athenians of course did not immediately agree to the arrangement. As was the custom at that time, they sent messengers to the island of Delphi to ask the Oracle for guidance. But the news they received from the Oracle was not very hopeful.

Upon the death of the young Cretan Prince, a plague was unleashed on Athens. The Oracle foretold that unless King Aegeus gave in to King Minos' demands, Athens would continue to be besieged by the plague. And so, the Athenians had no choice but to agree. The fate of the young men and women of Athens now lay in the drawing of lots.

Mourning but victorious, King Minos returned to Crete and awaited the tributes that Athens was to send. The Minotaur was to have its fill with the youths and maidens.

IV. The Death of the Minotaur

On the third year that Athens was to send tributes, King Aegeus' son, Theseus volunteered to go. He swore to his father that he would end the suffering of the Athenians by slaying the Minotaur. While the King didn't want Theseus to go, he finally gave in.

Theseus vowed that he would come home victorious. He told Aegeus to look to the horizon and await the boat that would bring him home. If he was successful then he would raise white sails so his father would know immediately that he was alive. If he was to perish, which he said would not happen, the boat would have black sails.

And so, the brave Athenian prince sailed to Crete with the rest of the tributes. He was a fierce fighter, so he was confident that he would be able to free his countrymen from the Cretan monster.

When the tributes arrived at Crete, King Minos' two daughters, Ariadne and Phaedra, saw Theseus. Despite knowing that the youth was headed to the Labyrinth to be fed to their half-brother, the Minotaur, they fell in love with the brave Athenian.

Ariadne's affections it seemed were not unrequited. Theseus promised that he would take her away from Crete and would wed her if he was to survive the Labyrinth. He was certain that he could overpower the Minotaur, but may not be able to find his way out. The grand Labyrinth was a maze of rooms and corridors and only the Minotaur knew its way around.

So even if he did manage to kill the beast, Theseus

lamented that he and the others would probably be lost in the Labyrinth for eternity. Stricken at the thought of losing her newfound love, Ariadne went to Daedalus to ask for his help. He was, after all, the one who built the Labyrinth.

The skilled architect took pity on young Ariadne and decided to help the two lovers. Being imprisoned by King Minos may have also played a huge factor in Daedalus' decision to help Theseus and Ariadne.

So, the creator of the Labyrinth gave Ariadne a ball of gold string. All Theseus would have to do was tie the end of the string at the entrance and unravel it as he went further inside. Ariadne quickly went to her Prince to give him the ball of string. She repeated the instructions Daedalus gave her and waited for her lover to return.

Theseus then went in with the rest of the tributes. But as others hurried to find hiding places, the brave Athenian Prince sought out the monster. He let out the string as he explored further. At the other side, towards the very end of the Labyrinth, Theseus found the Minotaur.

The accounts of how the Athenian beat the monster vary. Some say that Theseus won with his fists while others say that he was able to slay the Minotaur with a sword. But what's important was that Athens was finally free. Once the half man and half bull creature was dead, Theseus searched for his fellow tributes and they all used the string to find their way out.

Ariadne was overjoyed with her hero's return. And true to his promise, Theseus took the young woman with him and they set sail for Athens. They took with them Ariadne's sister, Phaedra, who was also in love with Theseus.

V. The Sad Homecoming

Minos was furious at his daughters' betrayal. He sent ships after the Athenians. But the gods were truly smiling down on Theseus as they were able to journey on unharmed.

But sadly, Ariadne was not to have her happy ending. On the way home, Theseus' ship docked at Naxos. With the numerous accounts of the story, it is not made clear whether Theseus had meant to leave Ariadne asleep on the island or whether it had been an accident.

The Cretans were still after the Athenian ship, so it may have been that in the rush to get back to Athens that Theseus had forgotten to wake Ariadne up and take her with them. Some say though that the decision to abandon the young woman was intentional.

Theseus was uncertain of the how the people of Athens would react to the news that he was to wed the Princess who had betrayed her own country. She had been instrumental in the death of her own brother and this might not have been something that the Athenians could accept.

And so, poor Ariadne had been left alone. Some stories say that when she realized that she had been abandoned on the island, she had been so devastated that she hung herself. However, there are stories that say she became the bride of Dionysius who took pity on the betrayed princess.

Theseus, on the other hand, sailed on. With Ariadne gone, he decided to take Phaedra as his betrothed instead. He eagerly awaited their return home to break the news to his father, King Aegeus, that the Minotaur was dead. There would be much celebration in Athens as no tributes would ever have to be sent again.

In his excitement, Theseus forgot his promise to his father. He was not able to change the sails of the ship. As they approached Athens, King Aegeus caught sight of the ship and the black sails that were raised. He was overcome with grief, believing that his beloved son had perished at the hands of the monster. So great was his grief that he jumped off a cliff into the sea and fell to his death.

Theseus was then crowned King of Athens. To honor his father, the brave hero named the sea where the King had fallen the Aegean Sea.

Medusa

I. Medusa, the Gorgon

Medusa is undoubtedly one of the most well-known Greek Mythology antagonists. She and her two sisters, Sthenno and Euryale, were known as the Gorgons. They were the children of the sea god, Phorcys (Phorkys), and his sister, Ceto (Keto). The Gorgons had other siblings from Phorcys that, like them, were monsters that were to be reckoned with. One of these siblings was the three sea hags called the Graiai who shared one eye amongst themselves.

Medusa, though, was a foe worthy of the bravest Greek heroes. While her appearance had been described as hideous, she wasn't always quite so terrifying.

Unlike her two sisters, Medusa was mortal and she was once an extremely beautiful woman. She had piercing eyes that men could not help but sing praises about. Her long lustrous hair rivaled that of the goddesses and many a suitor longed to run their fingers through her locks.

But Medusa would have none of it. Despite her numerous suitors, she chose instead to become a priestess at one of the goddess, Athena's, temples. Much to the frustration of the men who adored her, Medusa was unattainable. Priestesses at Athena's temple took a vow of celibacy and they were to remain virgins for their entire lives.

II. The Punishment of Medusa

While most of Medusa's admirers had given up on the virtuous priestess, there was one who would not take no for an answer. Poseidon, the sea god pursued the beautiful Medusa.

She ran to the temple to seek out the protection of Athena. She had thought that Poseidon would not touch of her if she was within the walls of the temple. But she was wrong. Blinded by his passion, Poseidon ravished Medusa in Athena's temple.

There are some versions of the story where Medusa is not taken by force. She falls in love with the sea god as well and instead of staying faithful to her vow of being celibate, she marries Poseidon. Whichever version one chooses to believe, the results were the same.

When the goddess found out what happened, she became furious. In her eyes, Medusa had defiled her temple. As punishment, she turned her vow-breaking priestess into a hideous being. The eyes that had once been admired by men became a curse to behold. Anyone who caught Medusa's stare would immediately be turned to stone. The beautiful strands of her hair were transformed into vile and venomous snakes.

Some stories say that despite the snakes and the gaze of stone, Medusa remained beautiful. Only this time, to look at her was deadly. Puzzling as it may seem, Medusa's punishment from Athena was deemed just.

Medusa lived with her sisters at the Western Ocean close to the Hespirides. There are tales though that say the sisters really lived in what is now known as Libya.

III. The Hero Perseus

After she was turned into a monster, Medusa stayed with her sisters. Stories about them spread far and wide, so heroes came from all corners of the world to slay them. But despite their skills with weapons, Medusa turned them all to stone. Medusa, it seemed, could not be defeated.

Now as it would happen, there was one hero who would come and end the Gorgon, Medusa. His name was Perseus. His life had not been an easy one and one of the quests that he was destined to complete was to kill Medusa.

Perseus was the son of Danae, the princess of Argos. Her father, King Acricius, had imprisoned her because of a prophecy from the Oracle of Delphi. When the King consulted the Oracle about his lack of male heirs, he was told that he would be killed by Danae's son. The princess then was childless. So, the terrified king decided to keep her locked up to stop the prophecy from being fulfilled.

Locked away and sad, Danae caught the eye of Zeus. The great god of the Skies took pity on the poor princess and went to visit her. He got into her prison by changing into golden rain. In this form, he was easily able to get inside the tower where the princess was held and straight into her womb. The child from that visit was Perseus.

King Arcicius was enraged when he found out that Danae was with child. He remembered the prophecy and feared that it would come true. Since Zeus fathered the child, there was no way that he could kill it. Doing so would put him at the mercy of the furies, and the wrath of the gods was not something to be taken lightly.

The King decided to send his daughter and grandson away instead, but he could not risk the child growing up and fulfilling the prophecy. So, he put the mother and child in a wooden box and cast them out to sea. He was sure that the pair would die out in the rough waters.

But Zeus saw what was happening. He called out to his brother Poseidon and asked him to calm the sea. So, instead of perishing, Danae and her son Perseus made it to the shores of Seriphos safely. They were given refuge by Dictys, the brother of the Seriphos king, Polydectes.

The King saw Danae and wanted to marry her, but he had no need for her son Perseus. Danae on the other hand did not want to become Polydectes' bride. So, in order to get rid of her son, the king threw a party. He asked each guest to bring a horse as a gift.

Polydectes' plan was to humiliate Perseus who came to the banquet without a gift. The young hero was quick to make a promise to the King. He pledged to the king that he would bring whatever gift the latter wanted. Polydectes thought it was a brilliant proposition.

IV. The Quest to Kill Medusa

King Polydectes demanded that Perseus bring back the head of Medusa. Since it was a quest that no hero had ever been able to do, he was sure that it was the perfect way to get rid of the young man. With Perseus dead, Polydectes would be free to marry Danae.

But Perseus was no ordinary hero: He was the son of Zeus. And he held the favor of the gods. Athena guided him on the quest by telling him to find the Hesperides. According to the virgin goddess, Perseus would find what he needed to slay the mortal Gorgon where the Hesperides lived.

But in order to find the Hesperides, Perseus needed to seek out the Graiais. These were the sea hags -- the Gorgon siblings -- who shared one eye. Perseus took the eye and demanded that the hags tell him where the Hesperides were. To stop the Hags from following him, Perseus took the eye with him.

With the information he got from the Graiai, Perseus was able to find the Hesperides. There he got a knapsack in which he could put the head of Medusa. He also got other useful weapons and tools to help him on the quest. Hermes gave him winged sandals that gave him the ability to fly. Hades' gift was a helmet that rendered the wearer invisible. This meant Perseus could get close to the Gorgons without being seen.

From Zeus, Perseus got a sword that he could use to slay Medusa. But it was Athena's gift that would be the most useful. The mortal Gorgon could not be defeated by the heroes who went before Perseus and this was because the minute they saw her they got turned to stone. To help Perseus, Athena lent him her shield which had a mirror like surface.

With all his gifts in hand, Perseus traveled to the cave of the Gorgons. There he found the statues of the fallen heroes who had tried to kill Medusa. These were reminders of the peril that he was about to face. Perseus used Athena's shield to find the Gorgons. He knew that of he saw Medusa with his own eyes, he too would be turned to stone. So, instead of looking straight, he used the shield's mirror like surface to search the cave.

Once he saw the reflection of the Gorgons on the shield, he quietly backed into the cave, taking care not to turn around. His steps were made lighter by Hermes' sandals so Medusa and her sisters did not hear him come close.

He reached out and took his father's sword out and beheaded Medusa. Once her head was cut off, a winged horse and a gold wielding giant sprang from her neck. The horse was Pegasus and the giant, Chrysaor. They were the children of Medusa and Poseidon.

Once the deed was the done, Perseus put the helm from Hades on. Medusa's sisters, the other two Gorgons tried to pursue him but because he was invisible, they were unable to see him.

V. The Head of Medusa

While Perseus had successfully killed Medusa, her power was far from gone. Her severed head could still turn people to stone, so it was a dangerous weapon to have. The young hero put it in the knapsack that he had gotten from the Hesperides.

On his journey home, Perseus stopped at Ethiopia to help the kingdom of Cepheus and Cassiopeia. Their land was besieged by the sea monster Cetus. Poseidon had sent Cetus to the kingdom to punish the Queen for claiming that the beauty of her daughter Andromeda rivaled that of the Nereids.

Nereids were sea nymphs known for their kindness and beauty. They were the daughters of the Nereus, a primordial sea god. Cassiopeia's claim enraged Poseidon as his wife was one of the Nereids. The mortal Queen had dared compare the beauty of her daughter to that of Poseidon's Queen.

When Perseus saw Andromeda, he could not help but fall passionately in love with her. To win her hand, the young hero slew Cetus. But Andromeda was already betrothed to another man. This resulted in a fight where Perseus took out his prized Gorgon's head and turned his rival into stone.

Perseus then continued with his journey home but before he got back to Seriphos, he passed by Atlas who stood with the sky on his shoulders. When the titan tried to attack him, the brave hero took out Medusa's head again. Despite already being dead, the Gorgon's stare turned the titan to stone, thus creating the Atlas Mountains.

There were also creatures that spawned from the severed head. Stories say that drops of Medusa's blood fell on the Libyan region and immediately turned to snakes. These drops were also where the vipers that killed the Argonaut, Mospos, came from.

Finally, after a long and eventful quest, Perseus was home. He then learned of how Polydectes had tricked him. To avenge himself and his mother, he took out Medusa's head and turned the King and his courtiers to stone.

With Polydectes gone, Perseus gave the throne to Dictys, the kind man who had saved them on the shores of Seriphos. With his quest completed, Perseus gave the head of Medusa to Athena who put it on her shield.

And so, while the mortal gorgon had been slain, her severed head still possessed the power she had been cursed with.

Heracles

I. The Son of Zeus

Heracles (Herakles) is the Greek name of the famous hero Hercules. He is known for his great strength and the numerous adventures he had. Heracles led a tough life because of his stepmother, the goddess Hera.

Herakles was the son of Zeus and Alcmene (Alkmene). Alcmene was the descendant of Perseus, another great hero who was also the son of Zeus. The god of the skies was passionately in love with Alcmene who lived in Thebes with her husband Amphitryon.

Both were originally from Argos but had fled after Amphitryon's brother was killed during one of their violent arguments. Zeus saw the beautiful Alcmene and vowed that he would have her. So, he tricked his way into her bed by taking on the form of her husband.

That union bore fruit. Alcmene became pregnant and Zeus once again was to have a son with a mortal woman. Another demigod stepson was more than Hera could bear. She knew that Zeus would bless this child and she would have none of it.

Zeus had made a decree that his son would be the ruler of the Mycanaean Kingdom. Amphitryon was the nephew of the King, so the son of Alcmene would have a claim to the throne. Hera, however, had a few tricks up her sleeve. She sent two witches to the mortal woman to delay the birth or even kill the child. But the servants of Alcmene found out about the witches.

So thought they were not able to kill the baby, the witches were successful in delaying the birth. They made sure that another child of the same bloodline was born first. As a result, Eurystheus, the other child, inherited the kingdom instead.

While Hera succeeded in taking away Mycanea from Zeus' child, it was born alive and healthy. Alcmene named her son Alcaeus. The baby had immense strength which was a sign that he was no ordinary mortal boy.

Alcaeus' name would later be changed to Heracles as he became famous for the challenges and difficulties that would plague him his entire life. Heracles literally means "Glory of Hera", so it basically foretold that Hera would bring about most of these trials in his life.

The resentful goddess was not done with Heracles. She was still set on killing her husband's illegitimate offspring. So, she sent two serpents to slither into the baby's cradle when no one was looking. She was certain that the snakes could kill the defenseless looking babe.

But Hera was mistaken. Even as an infant, Heracles already had unsurpassable strength. When the serpents slithered close to him, he reached out and strangled them both, thus killing them with his bare hands. Hera was furious, but she knew she had to bide her time before she attempted to kill him again. While she was a powerful goddess, she could not risk the wrath of Zeus if he found out what she was up to.

Another version of the myth told of how Alcmene brought the infant Heracles to the woods to keep him safe from Hera. Athena came upon the babe and brought him to Hera saying he was an orphan. The Queen did not recognize the baby and took him in her arms to nourish him. But while she was nursing him, Heracles bit the goddess. Hera pushed him away spilling some of her milk. This was how the Milky Way was created according to legends. Athena took the babe, who was now imbued with great strength and stamina from the milk he had nursed from Hera.

Heracles then led an uneventful few years with Hera leaving him in peace. He grew up at his stepfather, Amphitryon's, household. The mortal man thought the child was his own, so Heracles was treated well. He was given the best tutors where he learned how to shoot arrows, wrestle and play musical instruments.

One of his tutors was Apollo's son, Linus. Heracles, although physically immaculate, had quite a few weaknesses. He was quick to anger and it was during one of his uncontrollable tempers that he struck down Linus. His teacher fell down dead and Heracles was inconsolable.

As punishment, he was sent with the herdsmen to tend his stepfather's flock. Everybody thought that with him safely away, he could avoid trouble. But Heracles was attracted to trouble. While he was with the herdsmen, he heard about the Minyans (natives) who had attacked a group of Theban warriors. The latter lost and this Heracles found extremely unjust.

He left the flock and fought alongside the Theban warriors to avenge their earlier defeat. And with his superhuman strength, Heracles led the fighters of Thebes to victory.

Creon, the king of Thebes, heard about the brave young hero. He was grateful for the help in fighting off the Minyans. Creon noted that to have a man such as Heracles on his side was certainly a prize. So, as a reward and to keep the strong demigod's loyalty, he gave him his daughter Megara. The two were wed and it seemed that all would be well for the last son of Zeus.

II. From Alcaeus to Heracles

But Hera was by no means done with her husband's illegitimate son. She saw how happy he was with his wife and children. Seeing Heracles so content and happy did not sit well with the infuriated goddess. She sent a curse that caused the young hero to go mad, and during this moment of madness, Heracles slaughtered his family.

The rage the madness brought on continued and it seemed as though it would never end. The goddess Athena took pity on Heracles and knocked him on the head with a stone. Only then did the madness abate. Once he was back to his old self, he saw what he had done to his wife and children. So great was his guilt and grief that he attempted to take his own life.

It was his cousin, Theseus, that stopped Heracles from committing suicide. Theseus argued that it was the coward's way out and the right thing to do was to find a way to atone for his sins. The broken hero heeded his cousin's advice and sought out the wisdom of the Oracle at Delphi.

Apollo, the god that the Oracle served, understood that despite Heracles killing his family it was not entirely the hero's fault. Hera's anger towards the demigod was no secret. Apollo knew that the madness had been caused by a curse from the Queen of the gods. So, through the Oracle, he told Heracles to go to his cousin, Eurystheus, and complete tasks for him. Hera, of course, could not let this golden opportunity to make her stepson even more miserable pass her by. She influenced Eurystheus to choose the most difficult quests.

It was when he left Delphi to go to his cousin that Heracles became known by that name rather than Alcaeus, which his mother had given him.

III. The Nemean Lion

The agreement between Heracles and his cousin was for ten labors. But this would go up to twelve because of certain conditions that Eurystheus claimed Heracles was not able to fulfill.

The first of the labors was by no means an easy one. Eurystheus sent Heracles to slay the lion that terrorized the lands around Nemea and to bring back its skin as proof. This lion was said to have skin that was impenetrable so no sword or arrow could kill it. Heracles set out for Nemea eager to get the first quest done.

Since no weapon could kill or even injure the Nemean Lion, Heracles lured it into a cave where he cornered it and strangled it with his bare hands. He skinned the lion and travelled back to his cousin, wearing the lion's skin as a coat. This is why Heracles is depicted in most paintings and carvings as wearing a lion coat.

When Heracles got back to Eurystheus, the latter was terrified at what he saw. His cousin was able to defeat the lion that nobody else was able to kill. He refused Heracles entry to the town's gates and thereafter gave out the quests through a messenger. Heracles kept the skin of the lion which still retained its impenetrable qualities.

IV. The Lernean Hydra

The second labor that Heracles was sent to do was to slay the Hydra that lived in the murky swamps of Lerna. A hydra is a serpent like creature that has nine heads. Eight of the heads were mortal while one was immortal. In order to defeat the hydra, the mortal heads needed to be killed first. But there was one problem, every time one of the heads was cut off, two more would grow in its place. To make matters worse, there was another creature that helped the monster out, a crab.

On this quest, Heracles took along his nephew Iolaus. They travelled to Lerna where the brave hero lured the Hydra out of the waters. During the battle, the sea serpent coiled around Heracles' foot making it impossible for him to move away. The crab which fought alongside the Hydra kept biting the trapped foot.

Heracles called out to Iolaus for help. Every time he chopped or bashed one of the mortal heads, his nephew would hold a torch and burn the cut or bashed part. This prevented the Hydra from growing two more heads to replace the one that was defeated.

When Heracles cut off the last head, he buried it on the ground to keep it away from the body and stop the monster from respawning. He then cut into the body of the Hydra and dipped his arrows in its poisonous blood.

With the Hydra slain, Heracles and Iolaus went back to Eurystheus victorious. But the latter would not consider killing the sea serpent as one of the labors. This was because Heracles was helped by his nephew. This meant the hero still had 9 labors to go.

V. The Ceryneian Hind

For his third labor, Eurystheus sent Heracles to capture the hind of Ceryneia. Ceryneia was a town not far from Mycenae so the task may sound like an easy one. However, the hind, or female red deer, that Heracles was to catch had golden antlers and hoofs made of bronze. It ran swiftly so it was difficult to capture.

But what made this quest even harder was that the hind belonged to Artemis. This meant Heracles could neither kill nor injure the creature lest he risk offending the goddess of the hunt. With already one powerful goddess after him, Heracles did not want one more Olympian to vow revenge against him.

After an entire year, Heracles was finally able to catch the hind. He did so by shooting an arrow on its hoof. But on the way back to Mycenae, he met Artemis and her brother Apollo. The goddess was of course enraged when she saw the injured hind. She was about to punish Heracles when the hero told her his story.

Artemis pitied Heracles and showed him mercy. She healed the hind and let the hero take it with him back to Eurystheus so he could complete the third labor.

VI. The Erymanthian Boar

The fourth labor sent Heracles to a mountain called Erymanthus. Eurystheus asked his cousin to bring back the wild boar that wandered the mountains. It wreaked havoc in the villages surrounding the mountain as it would gouge the villagers and destroy everything in its path.

It was during this quest that Heracles fought with the Centaurs. They were attracted by the smell of the wine that Heracles had opened. As a result, he killed a few of the Centaurs who attacked him. He also accidentally caused the death of one Centaur who was his friend.

To capture the boar, Heracles chased after it until the beast got tired and hid in a thicket. He poked it out into the open with a staff and hurriedly caught it in a net. He then travelled back to Mycenae carrying the boar in the net.

VII. The Augean Stables

For his next labor, Eurystheus sent Heracles to King Augeas to clean out the famous stables. Augeas had a large number of horses and cattle which meant that the stables were always filthy. Because of the immense size, the stables were very rarely cleaned. Eurystheus commanded his cousin to clean these out in just a day. He figured it was an impossible task and one that Heracles would certainly fail to do.

But Heracles had a plan. He went to Augeas and offered to clean the stables. However, he said nothing about Eurystheus or the ten labors that he was supposed to complete as ordered by the Oracle. Instead, he asked to be paid for cleaning the filthy stables. The payment he asked was a tenth of the cattle that Augeas owned. The king was desperate to get this task done so he agreed. His son went with Heracles to make sure that the stables were indeed cleaned up.

Heracles then started on his labor. He knocked down openings on opposite sides of the stable. Once that was done he began to dig trenches around the two rivers that flowed nearby. With his immense strength and stamina, Heracles changed the course of the rivers and made them flow through the stables efficiently washing out all the filth.

With the task done, Heracles went back to Augeas. But the king had found out about the labors and Eurystheus, so he refused to pay the hero. Enraged, at being cheated Heracles left but vowed to return to get revenge.

Back in Mycenae, Eurystheus refused to count the labor that Heracles had just completed. He said since Heracles demanded payment it would not be considered as one of the labors he needed to complete to atone for killing his family.

VIII. The Stymphalian Birds

After Heracles cleaned the stables, Eurystheus vowed to come up with more difficult tasks. For the next labor, he sent Heracles to drive out the birds that gathered at a lake near Stymphalos. While driving birds away may seem easy compare to what Heracles had already done, the ones at Stymphalos were no ordinary birds.

One version of the myth says that the Stymphalian birds were man eaters and were just as vicious as leopards and lions. Not only were these creatures predatory there was also an immense number of them. Heracles was at wits end on how to complete the labor.

Athena came to the hero's rescue. She gave him a rattle like instrument called a krotala. It made such a loud noise that the Stymphalian birds were surprised and started flying away. Heracles then began shooting them down with his arrows.

IX. The Cretan Bull

The next labor Heracles was commanded to do was to capture the Cretan Bull. This creature featured in a lot of myths. The magnificent bull was a gift from Poseidon to King Minos who promised that he would sacrifice it back to the sea god. However, Minos went back on his word and decided to keep the beast. As punishment, Poseidon got the help of Aphrodite to make Minos' wife fall in love with the bull. As a result, she got pregnant and gave birth to the half human-half bull creature that was later called the Minotaur.

The Cretan Bull was also responsible for the death of Minos' only son, which had caused the feud between Athens and Crete. The story of the Minotaur is also included in this book.

After all the other labors that Heracles had done, capturing the Cretan Bull proved to be quite easy. He wrestled the beast to the ground and rode it back to Mycenae. Eurystheus, however, decided to set the animal free and it wandered about in Marathon terrorizing the scared villagers.

X. The Horses of Diomedes

The next labor of Heracles has a couple of different versions. In one, written by Apollondrus, Heracles travels to the territory of the Thracian tribes to find the Bistones. The King of that tribe was Diomedes. He had a herd of flesh eating horses that Eurystheus commanded Heracles to bring back to Mycenae.

Apollondrus related that Heracles did not travel alone but rather with a group of volunteers who wanted to aid him in this labor. He and his companions sailed across the Aegean Sea and landed on the shores on Bistonia. There they were able to overpower the grooms that tended the horses. Heracles then led the horses out to the sea. But the Bistones had found out what happened, so they raced after Heracles and his companions.

In the battle that followed, Heracles was able to kill Diomedes who he then fed to the horses to keep them settled until they reached Mycenae. And just like with the Cretan Bull, Eurystheus set the mares free.

XI. The Belt of Hippolyte

Eurystheus' next labor for Heracles was even more dangerous than the ones he'd done before. This time, he sent his cousin to the Amazons to get the belt of Hippolyte. She was an Amazon Queen and undoubtedly the strongest and fiercest warrior in her tribe. The belt that Eurystheus wanted had been a gift from Ares.

Heracles recognized that he would not be able to go against an entire tribe of Amazons so he had some friends go with him. Aboard a ship, Heracles and his Greek friends set sail for the land of the Amazons.

When they docked at the shores of the Amazon territory, Hippolyte welcomed them and asked why they had come. Heracles quickly told her about the labors he was to complete. The Amazon Queen sympathized with Heracles and promised to give him the belt.

However, Hera, who had watched the hero complete one labor after another, was not going to make the latest one easy for him. So she took the form of an Amazon and spread the rumor that Heracles and the Greeks were planning to take their Queen away.

Enraged by what they heard, the Amazons put on their armor and prepared for battle. They rushed to the shore where the ship was docked and where their Queen stood with Heracles. The hero saw the armored Amazons ready for a fight. He knew that there was most certainly going to be a battle. He drew his sword and killed Hippolyte who still stood close to him. He quickly took the belt.

A great battle then ensued. Heracles and his Greek companions were able to drive the Amazons back and sail away on their ship. However, instead of returning to Mycenae immediately, he and his companions stopped at Troy.

XII. The Cattle of Geryon

For his tenth labor, Heracles was sent to get the cattle of Geryon and bring them back to Mycenae. Geryon kept his cattle on the island of Erythia where they were guarded by a two headed dog named Orthus. This hound was the brother of Cerberus, the three headed beast of the underworld. The cattle were also watched by a herdsman named Eurytion.

Heracles' journey to Erythia was an eventful one. He encountered and killed quite a few wild creatures. But the most famous of all his feats while on his way to get the cattle was when he built the pillars of Heracles. He did this when he split a mountain in two so he could pass through. One half was on the side of Libya while the other was on the side of Europe. When he created the pillars, he also created the strait that passes through them which is now called the Strait of Gibraltar.

Once he got to Erythia, gathering the cattle was easy. He defeated Orthus and Eurytion and was on his way back to Mycenae in no time. But the journey back home was much more difficult. Two sons of Poseidon tried to steal the cattle but the hero killed them without much difficulty.

Heracles lost one bull at Rhegium. The animal had jumped off the ship. It swam all the way to Sicily and then headed on to a neighboring shore. The country that bull went to was named Italy after 'italus' which was the native word for bull.

Heracles went after the escaped bull and found it in the herd of a ruler named Eryx. Eryx was another of Poseidon's sons who refused to give up his prize without a fight. He challenged Heracles to a wrestling match. Unfortunately for him, the hero he had challenged was much too strong for him so he ended up getting killed.

Heracles took the bull and went back to Hephaestus where he had left the rest of the cattle. It seemed that he would be able to continue with his journey back to Mycenae. But Hera was not about to let her husband's illegitimate son complete the labor that easily. Just as Heracles was at the end of the Ionian Sea, she sent a gadfly to scare the cattle into scattering.

Heracles had to collect his prize once more. It took him quite a while to gather each of the cattle. He blamed the river he was on for all his troubles so he threw rocks into it to make it hard to navigate for others. Finally, he was able to get back to Eurystheus and complete the labor.

The King of Mycenae took the cattle and sacrificed them to Hera.

XIII. The Apple of the Hesperides

After ten hard labors with two not being counted, Heracles was not about to have an easy time with his eleventh labor. Eurystheus wanted the golden apples that were kept in a secret garden by the Hesperides. The apples were watched by dragon with a hundred heads named Ladon.

Eurystheus knew that it was impossible for Heracles to complete this labor as the apples belonged to Zeus. They had been given to the great god by Hera. And since Hera despised Heracles, there was no way she was going to let him get her precious apples.

Heracles' first problem was that he didn't know where the garden was. So he travelled to different parts of the world, searching for information that could help him. But that was not the only thing that he found. While travelling, he encountered one of the sons of Ares, Kyknos, who challenged him to a fight. Heracles was not one to back down from such a challenge, so he agreed. But right at the heat of their battle, a thunderbolt struck them and stopped the fight.

Heracles then continued on and ended up in Illyria. There he captured the old man of the sea, Nereus. He forced the sea god to tell him where the garden was. He seized Nereus and held on to him despite all the different creatures the old man changed to. Finally, Nereus succumbed and told Heracles how to get the apples.

Heracles knew where the garden was located so he travelled to where Nereus told him to go. But his journey was not about to become easier. He was stopped by Poseidon's son, Antaeus, who was famed to be unbeatable as long as his feet touched the ground. Heracles was challenged to a fight and of course the hero obliged. He lifted Antaeus off the ground and crushed him to death with his bare arms.

Heracles was then captured by another of Poseidon's sons. Busiris would have made Heracles into a human sacrifice but the latter escaped killing his captor instead.

The hero's journey now took him to Mount Caucasus where he found the titan, Prometheus. Prometheus had been punished by Zeus for stealing fire and making fun of the Olympians. His sentence was to be chained to the mountain where every single day the sun would scorch his skin and a huge nasty eagle would feast on his liver. At night, the eagle would fly off and Prometheus' liver would grow back. But the following day it would start all over again.

The titan endured this punishment for thirty years. Heracles saw poor Prometheus and killed the eagle. To show his appreciation, the titan told the hero how to get the apples. While Heracles knew where the garden was, he did not know how he could get the Hesperides to give it to him.

Prometheus told Heracles to visit Atlas and get him to get the apples. After all, the Hesperides were his children so they would willingly give it to him. Heracles heeded the titan's advice and sought out Atlas.

Atlas was another titan who was punished by the gods. He was sentenced to hold up the sky, a job that he obviously hated. Heracles went to him and asked him for his help. Relieved that he would be freed of his burden, Atlas agreed to help Heracles. So the brave hero took the weight of the sky on his shoulders and Atlas hurried off to get the apples.

As promised, the titan came back with the golden

apples. But as he approached Heracles and saw his old burden, he decided to trick the hero into holding up the sky forever. He said he would bring the apples to Eurystheus instead and come back when he was done.

Heracles knew that he was being tricked and decided to give the titan a dose of his own medicine. He readily agreed to let Atlas bring the apples. But he asked a favor before the titan could leave. He asked if Atlas could hold on to the sky while he fixed the padding on his shoulder as the weight was rubbing his skin raw.

Atlas agreed and set the apples on the ground. He took back the sky on his shoulders and was surprised when Heracles picked up the apples and left.

But despite all the trouble Heracles went through to get the apples, Eurystheus couldn't keep them. Since they belonged to gods, no mortal could possess them. Heracles had to give the apples back. Fortunately he didn't have to travel back as Athena took it for him.

XIV. Cerberus

Finally, Heracles only had one labor left and Eurystheus obviously left the most difficult for last. For his twelfth labor, the King of Mycenae commanded Heracles to bring Cerberus to him.

Cerberus was a monster that belonged to Hades. While often referred to as a hound, Cerberus was much more complex than that. He had three wild dog heads, a back of snakes and a dragon for a tail. Aside from his monstrous appearance, there was one other thing that made the task of bringing him back to Eurystheus difficult. Cerberus was in the underworld. He guarded the entrance of the kingdom of Hades.

Heracles knew that the quest would not be easy. While he might easily find his way into the underworld, there was no guaranteeing that he would be allowed to return to the land of the living.

So, the first thing he did was to seek out a priest named Eumolpius. The priest was the creator of the Eleusinian mysteries. These were rites that celebrated Demeter and Persephone. Being initiated into the mysteries guaranteed that a soul would have happiness in the kingdom of Hades. Heracles successfully learned the mysteries and began his journey to the underworld.

On his journey in the land of the dead, Heracles encountered monsters and other heroes. There's even a story about how he participated in a wrestling match. After travelling for a while, he finally made it to where Hades resided. He asked the god of the underworld for Cerberus.

Hades agreed to let Heracles take Cerberus with him but only if he was able to subdue it with his bare hands. The young hero agreed and went in search of the beast. He finally found the three headed dog in one of the rivers that flowed in the underworld. He seized the heads and wrestled it into submission. Despite the dragon tail biting him, Heracles would not let go.

Finally Cerberus was defeated. And as agreed on, Heracles was allowed to leave the underworld and deliver the beast to Eurystheus.

XV. The Other Adventures of Heracles

After his labors, Heracles was finally free to go. But Hera had not given up on making his life miserable. She once again struck him with madness and in his rage he ended up killing the prince of Oechalia, Iphitus. He once again sought out the Oracle at Delphi to ask for help. The Oracle told him that he would need to sell himself as a slave to atone for his sins. And so Heracles was back into servitude.

He was bought by Queen Omphale and brought back to Lydia where he served his new mistress. While she did not ask him to do dangerous labors, she did humiliate the hero by making him dress in women's clothing. He was also asked to do needlework along with the other women at court. Eventually, he became the Queen's lover and then set free.

Even after that, Heracles' adventures were far from over. He joined other heroes on an expedition to Troy. This was way before the Trojan War though. After they won the battle, Heracles' was called on by the Olympians to help fight the titans. Gaia had awoken her children and they threatened to overthrow the gods of Olympus.

Heracles was able to help the gods and the Titans were defeated. He had played a key role in the battle which resulted in the Olympians showing him favor. But Hera was still bent on making his life miserable.

While still weak from fighting the titans, Heracles went back to Aegeus to complete unfinished business. He had been cheated out of the cattle that the king had promised to give him so he returned to avenge himself. However, since he was still recovering from the battle against the titans, Heracles lost to Aegeus.

XVI. The Death of a Hero

While his first marriage had ended in tragedy, Heracles was to have another chance at love. He met the Princess Deianira and fought for her hand in marriage. He wrestled the river god Achelous for the beautiful princess and was victorious.

But the hero was not destined for much happiness. Heracles and his new wife lived in Calydon for a while. His father-in-law's court was a good place to be at. However, one day he accidentally killed one of the cup bearers. Heracles lost his temper and struck the man down. The king understood that it had been an accident, but Heracles could not forgive himself. So he took his wife away from the kingdom to settle elsewhere.

While they were travelling, they met a centaur who tried to rape Deianira. Heracles struck him down with one of the arrows that had been dipped in the Hydra's blood. The centaur knew he was dying so he decided to play a trick. He convinced Deianira that his blood was a love potion that she could use to make sure that Heracles would love her forever. The poor woman took some of the blood and kept it in a vial.

The centaur's blood of course was not a love potion. Since he had been struck down by the arrow, the Hydra's potion now flowed in his blood as well. So what Deianira kept was actually poison.

Heracles and his wife ended up in Trachis where they settled and began a family. But the hero was not content for long. He went to war against one of his old foes, Euryteus. When he defeated his enemy, he took Euryteus' daughter Iole as a concubine. Deianira heard about her husband's new conquest and feared that she would lose him to the new woman. So she took out the vial of the centaur's blood and drenched Heracles' shirt in it. She washed the shirt to remove the stain.

She sent the shirt to Heracles to wear during the victory festival. But as soon as he put it on, it began to burn his skin. Heracles tore it off quickly but the poison was now on his skin. He couldn't bear the agony and decided that death was better than suffering.

Deianira realized that she had been tricked and that she had poisoned her husband. So great was her grief at causing him agony that she went and hanged herself.

Heracles climbed up Mount Etna where he and some of his friends built a funeral pyre. Once it was completed, he lied down and bid his friends set it on fire. Zeus saw what was about to happen and took pity on his son. He commanded that only the mortal part of Heracles would burn, but that the essence that was godly would be taken up to Olympus. Hera was not happy but she was not about to disagree with her husband. And so, Heracles' was taken up to Olympus where he lived with the gods. Finally, his days of suffering were over.

Sources

Greek literature is vast and varied; the set of canon texts is very large. Edith Hamilton's 'Introduction to Classical Mythology' gives an in-depth overview of the Greek gods and the great stories about them, many more than have been retold in it's article. Robert Graves' collection "The Greek Myths" also retells many Greek myths and tries to place them in a wider anthropological and theological context; many other classical scholars praise his readability but argue with some of his conclusions.

The ending of Prometheus' tale above is based on Aeschylus' play *Prometheus Bound*. Eros and Psyche's story is told at length in Apuleius' book *Metamorphosis*. The tale of Oedipus and his children is taken from the Sophocles' plays *Oedipus Rex, Oedipus at Colonus*, and *Antigone*. The story of the Trojan War comes largely from Homer's *Iliad*, though the ending of the war is mostly drawn from Virgil's *Aeneid*. Orestes' story is the subject of dramas by Aeschylus, Euripides and Sophocles.

Most ancient stories told about Medusa depicted her as being born a Gorgon with hideous features similar to that of her sisters. However, she was the only one who was mortal. The story used in this book about Medusa being a priestess and being punished with snake locks and the stone gaze was based on latter accounts taken from stories told by Ovid.

The accounts of Heracles' journeys were based on the stories of Appolondrus . Heracles' death and acceptance at Olympus were taken from the stories written by the famous mythologist Thomas Bullfinch.

Free Kindle Books

Sign up to my newsletter for free Kindle books.

By joining my newsletter you will be notified when my books are free on Amazon so you can download them and not have to pay!

You will also be notified when I release a new book and be able to buy it for a reduced price.

You will also get a free **Spartans and the Battle of Thermopylae** book delivered to your inbox (in **PDF** format) that can be read on your laptop, phone, or tablet.

Finally you will also receive free history articles delivered to your inbox once a week.

Simply click the link below to signup and receive your free book:
https://nostramo.lpages.co/patrick-auerbach

CPSIA information can be obtained
at www.ICGtesting.com
Printed in the USA
BVHW041455011218
534529BV00014B/243/P

9 781522 715702